GOD IS FOR US

A KIDS BIBLE STUDY ON

BELONGING TO CHRIST

TRILLIA NEWBELL

MOODY PUBLISHERS

CHICAGO

All Scripture quotations, unless otherwise indicated, are from the ESV® Bible (The Holy Bible, English Standard Version®), copyright © 2001 by Crossway, a publishing ministry of Good News Publishers. Used by permission. All rights reserved. The ESV text may not be quoted in any publication made available to the public by a Creative Commons license. The ESV may not be translated in whole or in part into any other language.

Scripture quotations marked (NLT) are taken from the Holy Bible, New Living Translation, copyright ©1996, 2004, 2015 by Tyndale House Foundation. Used by permission of Tyndale House Publishers, Carol Stream, Illinois 60188. All rights reserved.

All emphasis in Scripture has been added.

This study is adapted from the author's adult Bible study, *If God Is For Us: The Everlasting Truth of Our Great Salvation* (Chicago: Moody, 2019).

Published in association with Don Gates, THE GATES GROUP @ www.the-gates-group.com.

Edited by Amanda Cleary Eastep
Interior design: Faceout Studios, Paul Nielsen
Cover design: Brittany Schrock
Cover design of rope copyright © 2023 by asiah/Adobe Stock (594815815). All rights reserved.
Author photo: Parker Plott

Printed by: Versa Press in East Peoria, IL, March 2024

Library of Congress Cataloging-in-Publication Data

Names: Newbell, Trillia J., author. | Newbell, Trillia J. If God is for us.

Title: God is for us : a kids Bible study on belonging to Christ : a 6-week
   Bible study of Romans 8 / Trillia Newbell.
Description: Chicago : Moody Publishers, [2024] | This study is based on
   author's adult Bible study 'If God is for us'. | Includes
   bibliographical references. | Audience: Ages 8-12 | Audience: Grades 4-6
   | Summary: "It's important that kids know what's true about God and
   themselves . . . to know what God has done and is doing for them.
   Focusing on Romans 8-one of the most studied and beloved chapters of the
   Bible-this study cements kids in God's most precious, life-changing
   promises"-- Provided by publisher.
Identifiers: LCCN 2023053178 | ISBN 9780802432193 (paperback) | ISBN
   9780802472823 (ebook)
Subjects: LCSH: Bible. Romans, VIII--Textbooks--Juvenile literature. |
   Salvation--Biblical teaching--Textbooks--Juvenile literature. | BISAC:
   RELIGION / Christian Education / Children & Youth | JUVENILE NONFICTION
   / Religion / Christianity
Classification: LCC BS2665.55 .N492 2024 | DDC 227/.106--dc23/eng/20240126

LC record available at https://lccn.loc.gov/2023053178Originally delivered by fleets of horse-drawn wagons, the affordable paperbacks from D. L. Moody's publishing house resourced the church and served everyday people. Now, after more than 125 years of publishing and ministry, Moody Publishers' mission remains the same—even if our delivery systems have changed a bit. For more information on other books (and resources) created from a biblical perspective, go to www.moodypublishers.com or write to:

Moody Publishers
820 N. LaSalle Boulevard
Chicago, IL 60610

1 3 5 7 9 10 8 6 4 2

Printed in the United States of America

CONTENTS

ABOUT THIS STUDY (READ ME, PLEASE)

I don't know about you, but often when I receive something like a new gadget or electronic device like a new cellphone, I skip the instructions and go straight to trying to put it together or trying to make it work. Almost every time I skip the instructions, I realize that I'm a little confused about how to use the item. Think about the next page or two as your instruction manual. It would be easy to skip it, but you will be glad you didn't!

What This Study Offers You

This study is unique! We will spend the majority of our time in only *one* chapter of the Bible. The first week we'll look at the major theme of the book of Romans, and then we'll read a few chapters that lead up to Romans 8. The rest of our time will be in chapter 8. For thirty days, or one month, you'll be guided through one of the greatest chapters of all time! Each day will include the following:

READ: The reading prompt may direct you to read a whole chapter in the Bible, but most of the time, you will read a few verses every day.

WRITE IT OUT: Writing out the verse of the day in this space will help you think of each word and maybe even memorize them.

START HERE: "Start Here" is always your first lesson of the week. It includes every verse that you'll study throughout that week. The "Start Here" lesson also introduces the study. Some days you will only read that day. In weeks 5 and 6, you'll continue on to the Day 1 lesson.

LESSON: This is where you'll learn more about the verses you read and wrote out. The lesson will help you understand, study, and apply the verses to your life. Each lesson will include a few questions for you too.

LET'S GO DEEPER: Here are your Bible study and application questions. This is where you'll think about the meaning of the verses. I'll ask questions to reinforce what you have just read. Some days will have more questions than other days. This is because when you study the Bible, some passages (sections of Scripture) may need more explaining than others.

Pray: Each day will include a prayer prompt. I will help get you started, and you can add your own words. If you don't know what to pray, turn back to this page and pray the Lord's Prayer, below. This is how Jesus taught His followers to pray:

Our Father in heaven, may your name be kept holy.
May your Kingdom come soon.
May your will be done on earth, as it is in heaven.
Give us today the food we need,
and forgive us our sins, as we have forgiven those who sin against us.
And don't let us yield to temptation, but rescue us from the evil one.
(Matt. 6:9–13 NLT)

BIBLE STUDY BASICS
(KIND OF THE ABCs)

Step #1: Read the Chapter (or Book) Straight Through in One Sitting

The Bible is the inspired Word of God (1 Cor. 2:12–13; 2 Tim. 3:16–17), but it is also a book! So, I encourage you to begin your study of any part of the Bible by simply reading it that way—like a book. Feel free to write down certain themes you see, repeated words, and words you don't understand, but don't get bogged down in the details.

In fact, if you have time, I suggest that you begin by reading the entire book of Romans straight through. This will give you a sweeping overview of this powerful letter, which certainly wasn't divided into chapters and verses when Paul sent it to the Christians in Rome. Although we will spend the bulk of our time in chapter 8, knowing what is going on elsewhere in Romans will provide a helpful perspective.

But don't worry if you can't read the whole book. We will read one chapter a day to start before we jump into Romans 8.

Step #2: Explain the Context (Observe)

Have you ever walked up to some friends talking or overheard a conversation that seemed weird? I have. Once I walked up to a conversation already in progress and heard a woman say she had thrown a cat out of a window. I was so confused. But I quickly discovered that, in context, her statement made sense. She had thrown a stuffed toy out a window and down to a little girl. Whew, that explains it!

Other words for context are: background, situation, and conditions. It's what is going on in and around the thing you are reading. Think about your favorite book or movie. The context might include where the story took place. For example, Narnia is a place in *The Lion, the Witch and the Wardrobe* by C. S. Lewis. The fact that it was so cold in Narnia was important to the story. I won't give anything away just in case you haven't read the book. But knowing the context of the book matters.

Knowing the context of that conversation about the "cat" helped me a lot—and explaining context helps us understand Scripture as well. In this study, we will spend time understanding the context of Romans 8. Understanding the context will make the meaning all the more special and awesome!

What kind of context are we looking for when it comes to Bible study? For any book or passage, we need to consider:

- Who wrote it?

- When was it written?

- Who was it written for (the audience)?

- Why was it written (its purpose)?

- What was going on with God's people and the world in general when it was written?

- How does it relate to other parts of God's Word?

Step #3: Consider What the Passage Says—and What It Means (Interpret)

Once you have done those early steps, it's time to look for the meaning. Often the meaning is clear, but sometimes you may need to reread, think, and maybe even look up the words before you understand what it is saying.

This is a great time to compare a verse you are reading with other verses in the Bible. This is called cross-referencing. Your Bible may have little letters or numbers at the end of the verse. These match letters or numbers on the side or at the bottom of the page. Find those, and then look up the Scripture verse listed there. Cross-referencing can help you understand the meaning of the text. Looking at the text surrounding the verse you are reading also helps with both context and interpretation.

I always find it helpful to look for the gospel in the text—how it relates to Jesus and His saving work in the world. (Since the whole of God's story points to Jesus, you can do this even with Old Testament texts.)

Step #4: Apply the Text to Your Life (Apply)

The Bible's message is meant to be lived as well as read, so look closely for what God is telling you through His Word. Sometimes the application (what you should do, how you should think) will leap off the page. Other times, you might have to reread the text, think about it for a long time, and pray about it. That's okay. The more time you spend in the Word, asking the Holy Spirit to help you understand it, the more you'll find yourself turning to it.

During the first week, you'll get a chance to apply some Bible study basics on your own. I've simplified it into a common study form called: Observe, Interpret, and Apply.

Here's what you will do:

OBSERVE: Ask questions like who, what, when, where, and why: Who is the author writing to? What is happening during that time or in the passage? When was it written? Where was it written and where was the letter sent? Why was the letter written? Write out your answers.

INTERPRET: What does the text mean? Summarize it in your own words. Look for repeated words and then look up the meaning of any words you may not know. What's the context? Is there anything about the book of Romans that you've learned that will help you understand the meaning of the chapter? What did you learn in Day 1 or 2 that might help you understand why Paul wrote this chapter? How does it relate to the rest of Scripture? Is there anything that you've read in your Bible that reminds you of this chapter? What does the text say about God or about Jesus? Write out your answers.

APPLY: What is God's Word saying for you today? Write out your answer and pray for the Lord's help to do what you have learned.

I always make sure to ask: What does the text say about the character of God and/or how does it point to Jesus? Write out your answer.

During our study of Romans 8, I'll ask questions that will help you understand the context right away. Then much of our work will be on interpretation and application.

Let's get started!

WEEK

ONE

START HERE:
NO GREATER MESSAGE

Romans 8 is the chapter we're studying, but it's in the middle of a big book of the Bible. So, before we can really understand what we read in chapter 8, we will need to know what the *whole* book is about. Before we dive into Romans 8, let's get to know the book of Romans. Romans is a cherished book, and Romans 8 is a favorite chapter!

The book of Romans was written by Paul to the churches in Rome. Most people agree that he likely wrote the letter while spending three months in the city of Corinth (see Acts 20:2–3). Although Paul was a Jew, he wrote the letter in Greek, a language understood in those days by Jews and Gentiles alike. Like most of his letters to churches, this letter addresses issues that would concern the particular church it was addressed to.

Most Bible teachers agree that the gospel and the glory of God are central themes. Paul wrote, "For I am not ashamed of the gospel, for it is the power of God for salvation to everyone who believes, to the Jew first and also to the Greek" (Rom. 1:16). And he had a desire to "preach the gospel" to those in Rome (Rom. 1:15).

Do you know the meaning of the word *gospel*? We are about to explore the message of the gospel to help us understand Romans 8.

The gospel can be seen throughout the book of Romans—so much so that Christians have often used the book as a tool for sharing the gospel with others.

Do you see how they explain the gospel?

_____

_____

Write what you think the gospel is in your own words.

_____

_____

_____

_____

We should pause here to recognize something important. Paul wrote this letter to the church in Rome, which means he was not speaking of preaching the gospel to non-Christians. He was writing to Christians. The gospel applies to all of the Christian life. In other words, you and I need to hear the gospel too—daily.

Also, keep in mind that the Christians at this time would have experienced punishment from others because they believed and talked about Jesus. This is called persecution. You will see how this context— that Christians were persecuted—applies to what we read in Romans 8. Verses like Romans 8:36—which speaks of being killed for Jesus' sake—would not only have been meaningful, but literally true! To be unashamed of the gospel could have been a death sentence. But as Paul reminded the Christians in Rome—and you and me as well—our suffering doesn't compare to the glory that will eventually be revealed to us (Rom. 8:18). More about that soon!

The book of Romans has been special to Christians throughout the centuries and has changed many lives. Even today, if you ask Christians what their favorite book of the Bible is, many would place Romans at the top of the list. And if you ask what specific chapter in the Bible has had the most impact on their lives, many would say Romans 8—and for good reason.

Praise God for who He is and thank Him that He is your heavenly Father. Ask God to do good things (whatever you wish to ask). Ask the Lord to help you understand what you are reading. Tell Jesus how you would like to grow (example: *Help me to be kind and forgive me for when I'm unkind*). Thank Jesus for all that He has done.

Since this is your first prayer of our study, here's an example of what you could pray:

You are an awesome God. Thank You that because of Jesus, I can know You and call You my heavenly Father. I pray You would help my friends feel better today. Lord, please help me to know You better. Help me believe in You. When I am afraid to tell people about You, help me trust You and tell others all that You have done. Thank You for coming to earth and living perfectly. Thank You for dying on the cross, taking the sins of anyone who would believe in You, and defeating death. You are risen indeed. Amen.

Remember you can turn back to the "What This Study Offers You" section and pray the Lord's Prayer.

UNDERSTANDING
THE GREAT MESSAGE

Although our study focuses on Romans 8, it is good to have a general understanding of what comes before it. This study focuses on chapter 8 and chapter 8 of Romans begins with the word *therefore*, which means that everything that comes before it is important and connected. We won't be reading Romans 1–7 together so it's important that we understand the big theme: the gospel! This lesson helps us understand the context for the rest of our time in the study.

READ ROMANS 1:16–17

Write out Romans 1:16–17.

_____

_____

_____

_____

_____

_____

Have you ever been afraid to talk to someone? Maybe you felt shy or bashful. Maybe you wanted to be included in a game, but you didn't want to ask. There are so many reasons why we don't speak up when we want something.

What word stands out to you in Romans 1:16?

_____

_____

_____

Can you define ashamed?

_____

_____

_____

The apostle Paul was not ashamed (or bashful) of the gospel. Do you remember what the gospel is? Paul was happy to tell everyone about the good news of Jesus. When we are not ashamed of the gospel, we will share it with other people.

The book of Romans has a lot to say about the gospel! Paul wrote, "For all have sinned and fall short of the glory of God" (Rom. 3:23). God is perfect, but we sin, and our sin separates us from God. But God's love is so amazing, He sent His Son, Jesus, so that we would no longer be separated from God. Jesus lived a perfect life, but when the time came, He died on the cross and rose from the grave.

Jesus paid for our sins—He took all the consequences. Because of what He did, we can now have a relationship with God—our sins are forgiven. When you accept Jesus' free gift of forgiveness, you join His family. The Bible says, "But to all who did receive him, who believed in his name, he gave the right to become children of God" (John 1:12). The gospel is good news!

Did you know that someone shared the good news with me? That is how I became a Christian.

A young girl listened to me as I told her all the wrong things I had done. She was kind, and when I was done talking, she knew what I needed. What I needed was a Person—Jesus. My sin separated me from God, and the only remedy for that was the saving work of Jesus on the cross.

My friend had many reasons why she could have been afraid to tell me about Jesus. I was older than she was and came from a different background. We hadn't known each other for long, so she could have been afraid. But none of these reasons mattered to her. Why? Because she was not ashamed of the gospel or afraid to share it.

Paul had even greater reason to worry about sharing the gospel than my friend did. He was well aware of the violent persecution that happened to people who shared the gospel in those days—after all, he had once been a persecutor (Acts 9:1–4)! But Paul, too, was neither ashamed of the gospel nor afraid to share it. Perhaps this is because both my friend and Paul knew the power of the gospel to change lives—their own lives first.

How do you think that the gospel changes someone?

_____

_____

_____

Why is this important?

_____

_____

_____

Do you think that if we know Jesus and have trusted Him to be our Lord and Savior that we should tell other people?

_____

_____

_____

There will come a time—if the time hasn't already come—when we will have the choice to either tell people about Jesus or shrink back in fear and say nothing. We might feel like we don't know enough to tell other people about Him. Or we might believe that someone may make fun of us. But if we believe the gospel is true . . .

- that God sent His only Son, Jesus, who was fully God and fully man;

- that Jesus lived a perfect life on earth, died on the cross, and then rose and defeated death;

- that Jesus is the way (the only way), the truth, and the life

. . . then isn't it selfish for us to keep this incredibly good, life-changing news to ourselves?

You and I can ask the Lord for strength and bravery to share the good news. Maybe you don't share because you aren't sure if you have placed your faith in Jesus. If you have not, you can pray right now to know Jesus. Grab an adult and ask them to pray with you. Ask the Lord to give you faith.

LET'S GO DEEPER

1. Who wrote the book of Romans? When was it written, and to whom was it written?

2. Can you write out Romans 1:16–17 in your own words?

3. Why does the apostle Paul say he is not ashamed of the gospel, and what might that mean for the rest of the book?

_____

_____

_____

4. What is the gospel or good news? (We are going to write out this definition a few times throughout the study. If we understand the gospel, we will understand the theme of the book of Romans!)

_____

_____

_____

5. What do you think it means to be ashamed of the gospel?

_____

_____

_____

6. In verses 16–17, what words describe how the gospel works and what it does? (Hint: salvation, believes, righteousness, faith.)

_____

_____

_____

7. Take a moment to think about your relationship with Jesus. When and how did you become a Christian?

_____

_____

_____

_____

_____

8. *Can you say with confidence, "I'm not ashamed of the gospel"? If so, why? If not, what's making you ashamed, uncertain, or afraid to talk about it?*

PRAY

Praise God for who He is and thank Him that He is your heavenly Father. Ask God to do good things (whatever you wish to ask). Ask the Lord to help you understand what you are reading. Tell Jesus how you would like to grow (example: *Help me to be kind and forgive me for when I'm unkind*). Thank Jesus for all that He has done.

Prepare for Romans 8

The fun part of just studying one chapter of the Bible is that you get to focus on a few lines at a time for a whole week at a time! You are really going to understand and get to know Romans 8. But over the next few days, I want you to get used to reading larger sections of the Bible. If you want to grow in understanding one part, you must understand all the parts around it. So, for the rest of *this* week, you are going to read a chapter of Romans that leads up to our study of Romans 8.

ROMANS 5:
A LOT OF GOOD NEWS

READ ROMANS 5

Here are some basic Bible study questions you can use to better understand what you just read.

Observe

Who is the author writing to? **What** is happening during that time or in the passage? **When** was it written? **Where** was it written, and **where** was the letter sent? **Why** was the letter written?

Write out your answers.

_____

_____

_____

_____

_____

_____

Interpret

What does the text mean? Summarize it in your own words. Look for repeated words, and then look up the meaning of any words you may not know. What's the context? Is there anything about the book of Romans that you've learned that will help you understand the meaning of the chapter? What did you learn in Day 1 or 2 that might help you understand why Paul wrote this chapter? How does it relate to the rest of Scripture? Is there anything that you've read in your Bible that reminds you of this chapter? What does the text say about God or about Jesus?

Write out answers to as many of the questions as you can.

_____

_____

_____

_____

_____

_____

_____

_____

_____

_____

Apply

What is God's Word saying to you today?

Write out your answer and pray for the Lord's help to do what you have learned.

_____

_____

_____

_____

_____

Hint: Romans 5 includes a lot of great news. It also addresses the gospel, suffering, God's love for us through Jesus, our sin, and that Jesus' death on the cross was all that we needed to have a right relationship with God. Many of the things you just read you'll see again in Romans 8. So, if you don't understand words like *justification* or *justified*, don't worry. In your study of Romans 8, you'll spend a whole lesson just on that one word!

Praise God for who He is and thank Him that He is your heavenly Father. Ask God to do good things (whatever you wish to ask). Ask the Lord to help you understand what you are reading. Tell Jesus how you would like to grow (example: *Help me to be kind and forgive me for when I'm unkind*). Thank Jesus for all that He has done.

ROMANS 6:
THE POWER TO SAY NO!

READ ROMANS 6

Here are some basic Bible study questions you can use to better understand what you just read.

Observe

Who is the author writing to? **What** is happening during that time or in the passage? **When** was it written? **Where** was it written, and **where** was the letter sent? **Why** was the letter written?

Write out your answers.

_____

_____

_____

_____

_____

_____

_____

_____

_____

_____

Interpret

What does the text mean? Summarize it in your own words. Look for repeated words and then look up the meaning of any words you may not know. What's the context? Is there anything about the book of Romans that you've learned that will help you understand the meaning of the chapter? What did you learn in day 1 or 2 that might help you understand why Paul wrote this chapter? How does it relate to the rest of Scripture? Is there anything that you've read in your Bible that reminds you of this chapter? What does the text say about God or about Jesus?

Write out answers to as many of the questions as you can.

_____

_____

_____

_____

_____

_____

_____

_____

_____

_____

Apply

What is God's Word saying to you today?

Write out your answer and pray for the Lord's help to do what you have learned.

_____

_____

_____

_____

Hint: Romans 6 teaches us to say no to sin. Because we belong to God, we should live for God. Because we belong to Jesus, we now have the power to say no to sin! That means that when you want to yell at someone who made you mad, you don't have to. You can instead pray that God will help you. You can do that with all things. You and I don't have to obey our desire to sin. We can obey God.

Praise God for who He is and thank Him that He is your heavenly Father. Ask God to do good things (whatever you wish to ask). Ask the Lord to help you understand what you are reading. Tell Jesus how you would like to grow (example: *Help me to be kind and forgive me for when I'm unkind*). Thank Jesus for all that He has done.

ROMANS 7: WHERE YOU BELONG

READ ROMANS 7

Here are some basic Bible study questions you can use to better understand what you just read.

Observe

Who is the author writing to? **What** is happening during that time or in the passage? **When** was it written? **Where** was it written, and **where** was the letter sent? **Why** was the letter written?

Write out your answers.

_____

_____

_____

_____

_____

_____

Interpret

What does the text mean? Summarize it in your own words. Look for repeated words and then look up the meaning of any words you may not know. What's the context? Is there anything about the book of Romans that you've learned that will help you understand the meaning of the chapter? What did you learn in Day 1 or 2 that might help you understand why Paul wrote this chapter? How does it relate to the rest of Scripture? Is there anything that you've read in your Bible that reminds you of this chapter? What does the text say about God or about Jesus?

Write out answers to as many of the questions as you can.

Apply

What is God's Word saying to you today?

Write out your answer and pray for the Lord's help to do what you have learned.

Hint: We belong to Jesus. And because we belong to Jesus, we can grow more and more like Jesus. This is what it means to bear fruit. We know that we have sin because we have the Word of God and His perfect commandments, and we can see that we have not obeyed everything that He has written. It is good to know what we have done wrong, so we can grow and change and do what is right. How can we do what is right? Jesus! We thank God for Jesus and that He helps us do all that He commands.

Praise God for who He is and thank Him that He is your heavenly Father. Ask God to do good things (whatever you wish to ask). Ask the Lord to help you understand what you are reading. Tell Jesus how you would like to grow (example: *Help me to be kind and forgive me for when I'm unkind*). Thank Jesus for all that He has done.

Time for Romans 8

A Note from Me to You:

I'm so glad that you chose *God Is For Us* to help you read and study the Bible. As we are about to see, Romans 8 is a very rich chapter. There are a lot of big theological concepts and deep truths.

Theological might make you think, "Wow, that's a big word!" Theology is the study of God, so theological concepts and words help us know and understand God.

But here's why I really want to write to you. The book of Romans was written to Christians, and Romans 8 assumes the reader has already placed their faith and trust in the finished work of Jesus Christ.

So, if you need to go slow and read Week 1 again or talk through the gospel, do it! If you are reading it with a group, don't be afraid to ask your leader questions about what you are reading. If you're doing the study alone and find yourself confused or curious, ask an adult to help you understand. But more importantly, if you read and realize that you've never asked Jesus to be your Lord and Savior, you can ask Him right now. Even better, if there's an adult in your life who follows God, ask them to share more.

WEEK

TWO

START HERE:
LIFE IN THE SPIRIT

READ ROMANS 8:1–17

We have now entered our time in Romans 8! We will be here for the rest of our study. We'll begin with help from the Holy Spirit.

When TV shows or cartoons portray someone trying to choose between good and evil, they often show a little "devil" sitting on one of that person's shoulders and a little "angel" sitting on the other. It's kind of silly and certainly not real, but it does represent how you and I feel at times. It's as if there's one voice in our ear telling us the right way to go and another trying to lead us to do bad things. We feel the pull of trying to hear the right voice and walk the right way. It's not easy!

We are going to learn what it means to "walk by the Spirit" (see Gal. 5:16, 25). But we can only do that when we are strengthened by the Holy Spirit Himself!

But this isn't just a matter of choosing between our imaginary inner "devils" and "angels." It's a matter of learning to live in the strength and wisdom of our Savior. And for that, we are given a supernatural Helper— the Holy Spirit.

Isn't that incredible news? God doesn't call us to do something without providing what we need for the task. He calls us to obey Him, but He also helps us do it. And if we want to understand what God's Word says and understand how to rightly live for Him, we must ask God for help.

WHO IS THE HOLY SPIRIT?

The Holy Spirit is God who comes to live inside us when we trust in Jesus. He is our helper. If your brain is about to explode, no worries— most adults find this to be unbelievable and amazing too! To understand what it means to have "life in the Spirit," we must understand that we have the power to obey the Lord because we have the Spirit living in us. If we ask God to help us with anything—like when we ask God for help to love Him and to love other people—it is the Holy Spirit who gives us the strength to love. The Holy Spirit helps us remember God and do good things (John 14:16).

PRAY

Praise God for who He is and thank Him that He is your heavenly Father. Ask God to do good things (whatever you wish to ask). Ask the Lord to help you understand what you are reading. Tell Jesus how you would like to grow (example: *Help me to be kind and forgive me for when I'm unkind*). Thank Jesus for all that He has done.

NO CONDEMNATION

Write out Romans 8:1.

_____

_____

Can you define *condemnation*? Write it out:

_____

_____

Have you ever done something and felt bad about it? I mean really bad? I have! I remember when my sisters and I would fight over silly things like who got to sit in the front seat of the car. I would get angry if I didn't get to. Once I even called my sister a mean name. I didn't feel bad at first because I was still mad. But later, after I realized how silly I was being, I felt sad that I had done that to her.

To feel bad about sin is a good thing. That is called conviction. God in His kindness helps you and me see when we've done something wrong. It was wrong for me to be angry with my sister because I didn't get my way, and it was wrong to call her a bad name. At that moment, I sinned against God and against my sister. What I did next matters. If you and I have placed our faith and trust in Jesus, *when we ask God for forgiveness*, He forgives us completely!

God has made a way for us through Jesus to know Him and to be forgiven. But sometimes we don't believe that God forgives us. We might hide what we've done because we are afraid we won't be forgiven. There are times when humans are slower to forgive (or may never forgive). But not God. God forgives, and so we no longer need to be ashamed or scared.

To be condemned is a fearful thing. It means to be declared unworthy or even evil, to be judged and declared guilty. Think about a courtroom. In a courtroom, you have a judge, lawyer, and the person who broke the law. When a judge sentences that person and tells them they must go to prison, they are condemned or punished for what they did.

Condemnation is an expression of the strongest disapproval. It's not something any of us would want from anyone—especially God. All sin deserves condemnation. All the sin that you and I have committed and will ever commit deserves to be punished. But God poured out all the punishment on Jesus so that those who believe in Him would never experience punishment for our sin.

God tells us in His Word that there is *no* condemnation for those in Christ Jesus. That means that when God looks at you, He sees that Jesus has paid for your sin. God does not disapprove of you. In fact, His response to you is just the opposite. God not only approves of you; He even counts you as righteous because of His Son.

Can you define *righteous*? Write it out:

_____

_____

GRUDGES AND CONDEMNATION

Have you ever held a grudge against someone or had someone hold a grudge against you? I have experienced both. I've been upset with someone and made sure that they knew it every time I was around. They knew that I wasn't happy with them. I bet because of my actions, they felt condemned. I have also experienced someone's unforgiveness. God doesn't do that to us! When He forgives, He forgives completely.

Not only is there no condemnation, but God also doesn't hold our sins against us or deal with us based on our wrongdoing (look up Ps. 32:2 and Ps. 103:10). He doesn't hold a grudge. He is loving and could never do that. God doesn't remind us of our faults.

No condemnation doesn't mean there's *almost* no condemnation or just a little of it. *No* means none, zero, not an ounce of condemnation to be found because of Jesus.

1. Why is the word therefore *important to the first line of Romans 8? Can you define* therefore*? Why do you think that what you have read in Romans 5, 6, and 7 is important to understand as you read this verse: "There is therefore now no condemnation for those who are in Christ Jesus"? Do you remember anything from those chapters that we read earlier that would help you understand why there is no condemnation for those in Christ?*

Write your answers below:

Because of _____ that we read about in Romans _____ there is no condemnation for those in Christ Jesus.

2. Saying that "there is no condemnation for those who are in Christ" means that there is *condemnation for those who are not in Christ. What form does that condemnation take? Why are those who are in Christ not condemned?*

DAY 2: NO CONDEMNATION   39

3. *What does it mean to be "in Christ"? Write it out:*

_____

_____

_____

_____

Look up: Romans 6 and 2 Corinthians 5:17. Do you see any words that are repeated in Romans 6? Write out 2 Corinthians 5:17. After reading those Scriptures, what do you think it means to be "in Christ" now? Write it out:

_____

_____

_____

_____

_____

_____

_____

_____

4. *How does being "in Christ" help us understand "no condemnation"?*

_____

_____

_____

5. *Look at how you defined* condemnation *at the beginning. How would you change your definition now that you've studied Romans 8:1?*

_____

_____

_____

As you read Romans, you will learn much about God's attributes or character. You will see that God is kind and merciful. You will see that God is patient. You will discover so much about His love. As we read our Bible, we grow in our understanding and knowledge of God. That knowledge should lead us to worship Him and obey Him. As you read in the Let's Go Deeper section of "What This Study Offers You," we will take what we've been studying and think about ways to put it into practice.

Here are two ways you can apply Romans 8:1.

1. **Confess.** When you have done something wrong, you can admit it. You can tell the Lord through prayer and tell an adult in your life what you have done. Ask the Lord to forgive you. Then, ask Him to help you believe He has forgiven you.

"If we confess our sins, he is faithful and just to forgive us our sins and to cleanse us from all unrighteousness" (1 John 1:9).

2. **Forgive.** Because we experience forgiveness from God, we can extend that same forgiveness to others. When we are wronged, it can be hard to forgive. But because of Jesus and all that He has done, we can ask Him to help us learn to forgive. It won't always be easy, but it is good. We are more like Jesus when we forgive.

"If you forgive those who sin against you, your heavenly Father will forgive you. But if you refuse to forgive others, your Father will not forgive your sins" (Matt. 6:14–15 NLT).

Are there other ways you can put your faith in action? Write it out:

Praise God for who He is and thank Him that He is your heavenly Father. Ask God to do good things (whatever you wish to ask). Ask the Lord to help you understand what you are reading. Tell Jesus how you would like to grow (example: *Help me to be kind and forgive me for when I'm unkind*). Thank Jesus for all that He has done.

FREEDOM IN THE SPIRIT

READ ROMANS 8:2–4

Write out Romans 8:2–4.

_____

_____

_____

_____

_____

_____

_____

_____

_____

Let's define *law*. There are two types of "laws" in this chapter:

Mosaic law: This law consists of the commandments given to the Hebrew people through Moses in the books of Genesis, Exodus, Leviticus, Numbers, and Deuteronomy. The Mosaic law reveals sin, and it helped the Hebrew people know how to please the Lord. This law only reveals our sin; it doesn't free us from our sin.

Law of sin: Here the apostle Paul is not referring to the Mosaic law. (He will talk about that law in verse 4.) Instead, he is addressing the power of sin over our lives. He is referring to the power of sin that is within each of us. Sin separates us from God.

Read Romans 8:3. Write out the text in your own words:

_____

_____

_____

_____

You and I can try very hard to be perfect, but verse 3 helps us understand that only God can cleanse us of sin. No matter how hard we try, we will come up short because of the power of sin in our lives. On our own—in our flesh—we have no hope of pleasing a holy and perfect God.

But we don't have to try to do it on our own! Thank God for Jesus.

God sent His Son to do what the law could never do and what our flesh could never do. What is it that the law could never do and our flesh could never do? Save us! Only Jesus can rescue us from our sin. He is the only perfect One. He is the only One who could make a way for us to the Father—by making the ultimate sacrifice on our behalf.

You might be thinking, haven't we talked about the gospel already? Yes! Do you remember one of the main themes of the book of Romans? You'll see the good news from every angle as we walk through Romans 8. A fresh understanding of our need for salvation through Jesus will help us obey Him and enjoy Him.

Walking by the flesh means trying to get through on our own strength— we don't trust Jesus for our salvation, and then do the rest in our own strength. This leads to sadness, discouragement, and ultimately sin. When we walk in Him (or, walk by the Spirit), we put away our efforts to do it on our own. We trust Jesus for the rest of our lives—for every step of our Christian walk. Some results of walking in the Spirit are peace, kindness, forgiveness, and joy.

1. Why is it a good thing to have our sin revealed to us?

_____

_____

_____

_____

_____

2. Why do we need the Spirit to obey the Lord?

_____

_____

_____

_____

PRAY

Praise God for who He is and thank Him that He is your heavenly Father. Ask God to do good things (whatever you wish to ask). Ask the Lord to help you understand what you are reading. Tell Jesus how you would like to grow (example: _Help me to be kind and forgive me for when I'm unkind_). Thank Jesus for all that He has done.

SETTING OUR MINDS
ON THE SPIRIT

READ ROMANS 8:5–8

Write out Romans 8:5–8.

Have you ever worried about something? Maybe you had a test to take and you were nervous you wouldn't do well. Maybe you had to give a book report in front of your class. Some of you may have moved to a different town or school and worried that you wouldn't find a new friend. It can be easy to let our minds run away with scary thoughts!

It's no accident that Jesus commands us to love God with our heart, soul, *and* mind (Mark 12:30–31). I can safely say that most of my sin starts in my mind from what I think. I imagine that's true for most of us. We know how to act, and there are a number of things we likely wouldn't do just for fear of what others might think. But our minds are another story. No one sees what we are thinking—at least, that's the lie we tell ourselves. We can have bitter, angry thoughts; we can have fearful thoughts; we can be anxious; we can think poorly of others—all within our minds.

God knows every hair on our heads—and what's inside our heads too. He knows that we need not only help with what we do, but also help with what we think. Paul warns us that the mind set on the flesh leads to death.

Do you remember what "the flesh" means?

As we've already learned, this is because the flesh is rotten with sin. So, the mind set on the flesh is the mind set on sin. The mind set on the flesh isn't thinking about the things of God. It's not thinking about God at all!

What do you think it means to set your mind on the Spirit?

The prophet Isaiah wrote about the mind in Isaiah 26:3:

> You keep him in perfect peace
> whose mind is stayed on you,
> because he trusts in you.

What does Romans 8 tell us happens when we let the Holy Spirit control what we think? What does it lead to?

----

1. Do you believe that what we think is as important as what we do? Why or why not?

_____

_____

_____

_____

2. What is one way that you can let the Holy Spirit control you mind? (For example, you can pray when you are worried.)

_____

_____

_____

_____

PRAY

Praise God for who He is and thank Him that He is your heavenly Father. Ask God to do good things (whatever you wish to ask). Ask the Lord to help you understand what you are reading. Tell Jesus how you would like to grow (example: _Help me to be kind and forgive me for when I'm unkind_). Thank Jesus for all that He has done.

THE SPIRIT IN YOU

Write out Romans 8:9–11.

_____

_____

_____

_____

_____

_____

Did you write it out? It's great news to read that we aren't controlled by our sin (our "flesh"). We have power and can say no to the bad things we sometimes want to do.

Because we have the Spirit, we don't have to lie. We can instead tell the truth. Because we have the Spirit, we don't have to be unkind. We can love other people. Because of the Spirit, when we get worried, we can run to the Lord and ask Him for help.

Before becoming a Christian, I did not have the Spirit of Christ. (Christ was not in me, and I was not in Christ.) I did not belong to Him. Spiritually speaking, I was dead (Eph. 2:1)—dead in my sin. But God, who is loving and merciful, brought me to life. He gave me His Spirit and Christ's righteousness.

This is the experience of everyone who trusts in the finished work of Jesus Christ on their behalf. The Spirit gives us life because we have been made right with God! (v. 10).

Reread verse 11. Can you write it in your own words?

_____

_____

_____

The Spirit that is in us is the same that raised Jesus from the dead. Amazing! Have you heard of the resurrection? It's why we celebrate Easter. Jesus died and rose from the dead on the third day. The resurrection shows God's power to defeat sin and death. The same power that raised Christ is the same power that gives us life, too, and one day, we will live forever with Jesus.

LET'S GO DEEPER

1. The beginning of this verse includes a transition word. In the ESV Bible translation, the word is "however." In the NLT Bible translation, the word is "but." Why does Paul use the word however *or* but *in verse 9? (Note: To answer these questions, you may need to go back and read the verses before this one.)*

_____

_____

_____

_____

2. Knowing that the Spirit of God lives in you, how does that change the way you think and the things you do?

_____

_____

_____

_____

3. Bonus study: Read 1 Corinthians 15:35–38 and Philippians 3:20–21. How do these passages add to what Romans 8:11 has to say about our resurrected bodies?

PRAY

Praise God for who He is and thank Him that He is your heavenly Father. Ask God to do good things (whatever you wish to ask). Ask the Lord to help you understand what you are reading. Tell Jesus how you would like to grow (example: *Help me to be kind and forgive me for when I'm unkind*). Thank Jesus for all that He has done.

Here's an example of what you can pray:

Lord, thank You that You are my Father. You are an awesome and good God. I pray that I would not be afraid to tell You when I've done something wrong. And once I share it, I pray that I would trust that You have forgiven me. Thank You that because of You, Jesus, there is no condemnation for my sin; there's only forgiveness. It's in Your name I pray. Amen.

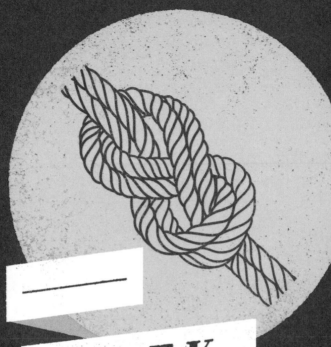

WEEK

THREE

START HERE: HEIRS WITH CHRIST—GOD'S CHILDREN

READ ROMANS 8:12–17

Living according to the flesh leads to bad things. The Bible tells us it leads to death. This is not talking about a physical death. Rather it's talking about a spiritual death. Living by the flesh means that we are not obeying God. But life in the Spirit leads to just that—life. Why should we want to live our lives by the Spirit? Because we are God's children! We should choose to listen to and follow our great God. We have been "bought" with a great price, so we are no longer slaves to sin. We are heirs with Christ. And one day we will join in His reign.

So, let's learn what it means to be "heirs with Christ" and "children of God."

PRAY

Praise God for who He is and thank Him that He is your heavenly Father. Ask God to do good things (whatever you wish to ask). Ask the Lord to help you understand what you are reading. Tell Jesus how you would like to grow (example: *Help me to be kind and forgive me for when I'm unkind*). Thank Jesus for all that He has done.

OBLIGATED TO THE SPIRIT

Write out Romans 8:12–13.

_____

_____

_____

Do you notice the transition word? What is it?

_____

Have you ever been really upset and thought, "I have to cry?" There wasn't anything you could do to keep yourself from crying. You tried hard to stop, but the tears came rolling down your face anyway. Crying isn't a sin, but similarly, sin has a way of making us feel "obligated" to it too. Think about a time you've been angry and you felt like you *had* to scream at your sibling. Or a time when you didn't obey your parent, and to get away with it, you felt you *had* to lie. Sin has a way of making us feel obligated to it. *Obligated* means that we are committed to it. Another word might be *required*. We feel like we must do something. But unlike our tears, which just come at times, we can control whether we act out in sin or not.

We see in Romans 8:12 that we are under obligation (the ESV translation says "debtors") to the Spirit. We do not have to do bad things because we have the Spirit and are ruled by the Spirit. We have no obligation to the flesh. And that means we can say no to sin.

The apostle Paul, writing to the Corinthian church, puts this another way in 1 Corinthians 10:13. "No temptation has overtaken you that is not common to man. God is faithful, and he will not let you be tempted beyond your ability, but with the temptation he will also provide the way of escape, that you may be able to endure it."

This scripture tells us two things: 1) we will be tempted to sin, and 2) we will always have a way out, a way to say no. We can say no because of Jesus' death and resurrection. So, next time you feel like you must give in to something you know you aren't supposed to do, ask the Lord for help, and remember you have the Holy Spirit. You and I can say no.

LET'S GO DEEPER

1. Think about what we learned in Week 2. Why are we "obligated" to live according to the Spirit? (Note: The answer to why the transition word was used is also the answer to this question.)

_____

_____

_____

_____

_____

2. Think of a time when you a) gave in to sin because you felt there was no way out, or b) were tempted to sin but experienced the way of escape. What happened? What did you learn from this experience?

_____

_____

_____

_____

_____

_____

_____

Praise God for who He is and thank Him that He is your heavenly Father. Ask God to do good things (whatever you wish to ask). Ask the Lord to help you understand what you are reading. Tell Jesus how you would like to grow (example: *Help me to be kind and forgive me for when I'm unkind*). Thank Jesus for all that He has done.

CHILDREN OF GOD, LED BY THE SPIRIT

READ ROMANS 8:14

Write out Romans 8:14.

_____

_____

Did you know that if you are a Christian, you are a child of God? You might be thinking, "Wait, I already have parents or guardians. How can I be one of God's children?"

Here are some verses calling God our Father:

"Yet for us there is one God, the Father, from whom are all things and for whom we exist, and one Lord, Jesus Christ, through whom are all things and through whom we exist." (1 Cor. 8:6)

"One God and Father of all, who is over all and through all and in all." (Eph. 4:6)

"Father of the fatherless and protector of widows is God in his holy habitation." (Ps. 68:5)

"But now, O Lord, you are our Father; we are the clay, and you are our potter; we are all the work of your hand." (Isa. 64:8)

"Every good gift and every perfect gift is from above, coming down from the Father of lights, with whom there is no variation or shadow due to change." (James 1:17)

"Jesus said to him, 'Have I been with you so long, and you still do not know me, Philip? Whoever has seen me has seen the Father. How can you say, "Show us the Father"? Do you not believe that

I am in the Father and the Father is in me? The words that I say to you I do not speak on my own authority, but the Father who dwells in me does his works. Believe me that I am in the Father and the Father is in me, or else believe on account of the works themselves.'" (John 14:9–11)

"See what kind of love the Father has given to us, that we should be called children of God; and so we are. The reason why the world does not know us is that it did not know him." (1 John 3:1)

"And the Word became flesh and dwelt among us, and we have seen his glory, glory as of the only Son from the Father, full of grace and truth." (John 1:14)

God is our Father. If you are a Christian, you now belong to God the Father.

The fact that Christians are added to the family of God and become His beloved children is one of the most amazing things to me. My earthly father was very cool. He loved his children. But my dad, even though I love him so much, doesn't compare to my heavenly Father.

God is perfect. My dad was not perfect. God is always there for me, no matter what. My dad tried to be there for me, but he couldn't always be there. The Scriptures say that there's no one like our God, our Father (Deut. 3:24).

I submitted to and obeyed my earthly father. I respected his authority in my life. Of course, I didn't do this perfectly (hardly!). But when my dad would say something, I usually listened. That was one sign that he was my father!

In a greater way, as we are led by the Spirit to obey God, our obedience is evidence that we are His. We aren't going to do it perfectly, but our desire to obey comes from Him.

Earlier, I talked about how it feels when we want to do something wrong. Well, because of the Spirit, we also do the right things. So, when you get angry and you decide not to yell, it's because God is helping you! Because you are not your own. You've been bought with a price, and you are being reassured of that through the Spirit within you.

Likewise, God treats us as His very own. The book of Hebrews reminds us that we are truly children of God (Heb. 12:8). This means that He not only gives us good things, but also disciplines us as He reveals sin and restores and rescues us just as a loving earthly father would. The Spirit helps us accept and respond to our Father's work in our hearts.

Today, if you sense that nudge in your spirit or a lot of joy—rejoice in knowing that you are a true child of God. Ask God to make clear the good and righteous steps to take, being led by the Spirit as you walk in a manner worthy of the gospel.

LET'S GO DEEPER

1. Have you ever thought of God as your father? How does that change the way you think about God?

2. Have you ever felt—or do you often feel—the "nudges" I mentioned? Describe a time in your life when you felt this.

3. What do you think it means to be led by the Spirit?

Praise God for who He is and thank Him that He is your heavenly Father. Ask God to do good things (whatever you wish to ask). Ask the Lord to help you understand what you are reading. Tell Jesus how you would like to grow (example: *Help me to be kind and forgive me for when I'm unkind*). Thank Jesus for all that He has done.

WE CAN CRY OUT TO OUR ABBA FATHER

READ ROMANS 8:15

Write out Romans 8:15.

_____

_____

What an interesting verse! Write it in your own words:

_____

_____

_____

To the first-century church, this reminder of freedom from slavery would be very important. Slavery was a reality in that culture, so people in that day would instantly understand the analogy of being released from slavery and not being pulled back into it. They knew there was a big difference between being a slave in someone's household and being a free member of the family!

We may not see slavery on a daily basis anymore, but Paul's analogy still holds powerful truth for us. We were once slaves to our sin (Rom. 6:20), but once we're a part of God's family, this is no longer true. Now, we are not only free, but children of Almighty God. And not only children, but children loved deeply by our Father.

It is no small thing that we can use the word *Abba* as we cry out to our Father. This Aramaic word for "father" is an intimate term, even somewhat childlike—children in Jerusalem today use the term *Abba* when they talk to their earthly fathers. It is also the name Jesus used in addressing God.[1] Because of God's grace, we can call God by the same name Jesus does! We belong to God's family the same way we can belong in our own family.

When you are fearful, you can cry out to your Abba Father, and He will hear you. Remember that you are His, that you've been bought with a price. And that means you are truly free.

LET'S GO DEEPER

1. How might understanding that we can call God our Abba impact how we approach Him? Do you feel comfortable approaching Him in such an intimate way? Why or why not?

_____

_____

_____

2. Read Mark 14:36. What does it mean that we get to use the same name for God our Father that Jesus tenderly used in the garden of Gethsemane?

_____

_____

_____

PRAY

Praise God for who He is and thank Him that He is your heavenly Father. Ask God to do good things (whatever you wish to ask). Ask the Lord to help you understand what you are reading. Tell Jesus how you would like to grow (example: *Help me to be kind and forgive me for when I'm unkind*). Thank Jesus for all that He has done.

---

1. Leon Morris, *The Epistle to the Romans* (Grand Rapids, MI: Eerdmans, 1988), 315; Douglas J. Moo, *The Epistle to the Romans*, New International Commentary on the New Testament (Grand Rapids, MI: Eerdmans, 1996), 502.

THE SPIRIT PROVIDES ASSURANCE

READ ROMANS 8:16

Write out Romans 8:16.

_____

_____

This text tells us that the Spirit confirms to us that we are children of God. The Spirit bears witness with our spirit to prove that it is true. How does this work? Let me ask you a few questions:

- *Have you ever been so sad that you asked your mom or dad to pray for you?*

- *Have you ever done something wrong and then asked God for forgiveness?*

There are other questions I could ask. But if you've answered yes to either of these, then it's likely your spirit—led by His Spirit—is saying to you, "Daughter or son, you are His." You can do this because the Holy Spirit is in our hearts (2 Cor. 1:22). This is such a wonderful reminder that we are His.

Today, with confidence and assurance, cry out to your Father. Even the greatest fathers on this earth do not compare with our Abba Father.

If you ever find yourself wondering where you belong, remember that if you have accepted Jesus, you belong to God the Father. You are His, and He is yours. There's nothing else you need.

1. To bear witness can be defined or described as to show that something exists or is true. What does it mean that the Spirit bears witness?

_____

_____

_____

2. Have you ever struggled to have the confidence to talk to God through prayer? If so, why?

_____

_____

_____

_____

PRAY

Praise God for who He is and thank Him that He is your heavenly Father. Ask God to do good things (whatever you wish to ask). Ask the Lord to help you understand what you are reading. Tell Jesus how you would like to grow (example: *Help me to be kind and forgive me for when I'm unkind*). Thank Jesus for all that He has done.

WEEK

FOUR

START HERE: FUTURE GLORY

READ ROMANS 8:18–27

Talking about suffering can be really hard. Suffering is anytime we experience pain, sadness, or a situation that causes hardship. The tough thing is, we will all experience it. There will be suffering until the day when we are with Jesus forever. Our verses today tell us that God's creation waits with groaning until all is perfect again. Don't you wish for the day when no one will experience pain and sadness? We have a hope—Jesus—and He won't put us to shame (we'll learn what this means this week!). Our great Hope understands our weaknesses and sent the Helper to assist us in our need. We are weak, but He is strong. We cry out, and He will answer in our day of trouble.

PRAY

Praise God for who He is and thank Him that He is your heavenly Father. Ask God to do good things (whatever you wish to ask). Ask the Lord to help you understand what you are reading. Tell Jesus how you would like to grow (example: *Help me to be kind and forgive me for when I'm unkind*). Thank Jesus for all that He has done.

INCOMPARABLE GLORY

READ ROMANS 8:18–19

Write out Romans 8:18–19.

_____

_____

_____

I have a friend who got hit by a bus. Yes, you read that right. And she not only got hit by that bus, she survived to tell about it. I won't reveal her name or tell her story. That is her own story to tell. But one of the things that was remarkable to me was watching her work through the suffering and pain—literal, physical pain—that followed her accident.

My friend focused on other people during much of her recovery! Isn't that neat? She would ask friends to pray for others who were suffering in the hospital rooms next to hers. She would thank God and share about how good He was during that time. And one time, she even joked about being hit by a bus, pointing out how often we use the phrase, "I feel like I've been hit by a bus," and it had actually happened to her!

Everyone suffers differently, and even as I reflect on my friend's response to her suffering, I want to make it clear that we are all free to experience our own pain differently. We don't have to be cheerful. As a matter of fact, many of the psalms help us learn to lament (or mourn) with sorrow and weeping. As we'll see throughout this week of study, even nature is groaning as it waits for the Lord's return.

It wasn't that my friend was faking her happiness. There was something deeper going on in her spirit. She was suffering with joy. She had taken to heart the reality that no matter how we respond to our suffering, none of it compares to the joy we can look forward to if we are in Christ.

Have you ever had a hard day and thought it was the end of the world or the worst thing ever? Suffering has a way of making us forget that one day we won't suffer anymore.

So, if the Word tells us that our suffering doesn't compare to the glory (heaven) that will be revealed, why don't you and I take a moment to compare?

SUFFERING	GLORY
We suffer because of our sin.	We will be sinless.
We suffer because of the sins of others.	Evil will not exist, so there will be no more sin.
We suffer from worry and anxiety.	There will be nothing to worry about, and our risen bodies and minds will never experience anxiety again.
We suffer because of sickness.	There will be no more sickness.
We suffer from living in a fallen world where we are subject to natural disasters.	There will be a new heaven and a new earth. No more earthquakes, tornadoes, lightning strikes, or hurricanes.
We suffer because of sadness.	There will be no more tears.
We suffer because of death.	No one will ever die (again).

Heaven will be amazing! You and I were made for glory—for heaven. And knowing *that* can help us as we suffer today. Paul tells us clearly that our present suffering doesn't compare to the glory we will one day experience. Knowing this future glory allows us to suffer well—in other words, we suffer with hope.

Today, by God's grace and through His Spirit, remember that your future isn't just bright—it's glorious! Glory awaits you at the end of your suffering.

1. Have you ever experienced a circumstance that felt confusing and hard? How did you respond to the situation?

_____

_____

_____

_____

_____

2. Do you ever get sad about circumstances that you have heard or seen? Maybe it's a sick friend or watching a war break out in another country, or maybe it's something that you've experienced. When you think about those things, does it make sense that "creation is eagerly waiting" for heaven?

_____

_____

_____

_____

_____

3. How might knowing our future glory help us when we suffer?

_____

_____

_____

_____

_____

4. *The biblical concept of glory might be hard for us to comprehend if we only look at the English dictionary. For example, the English word glory might mean to take pride or pleasure in something. But the Greek word translated glory in the context of Romans 8 means the bliss of heaven. In other places in Scripture, it means the fullness of God. How does the biblical definition of glory help us read Romans 8:18–19 differently? Rewrite these two verses, substituting the definition of the word glory.*

---

5. *List areas in your life that bring you suffering now but that will be healed by this future grace. Be as specific as you can—not just "broken relationships" (for example), but "my relationship with Mom"; not just "sickness," but "my asthma"; not just "injustice," but "I got in trouble for something I didn't do." Be happy in knowing that these things will one day be healed or restored (be made right).*

PRAY

Praise God for who He is and thank Him that He is your heavenly Father. Ask God to do good things (whatever you wish to ask). Ask the Lord to help you understand what you are reading. Tell Jesus how you would like to grow (example: *Help me to be kind and forgive me for when I'm unkind*). Thank Jesus for all that He has done.

HOPE FOR WHAT WE DO NOT SEE

READ ROMANS 8:23–25

Write out Romans 8:23–25.

_____

_____

_____

_____

_____

_____

How often do you say or think the word *hope* in a single day?

"I hope to see you soon."

"I hope I remember to bring my homework home."

"I hope I make the team."

"I hope my mom doesn't find out what I did."

"I hope I get a good grade."

Most of us spend a little time hoping for something. We do it without even realizing it. Have you ever said you hoped that something would or wouldn't happen?

The Bible has a lot to say about hope. The hope we find in Scripture— including the hope we find in Romans 8:23–25—is of something good. And it's a hope we can count on, unlike a lot of our earthly hopes and dreams.

You and I might fall into a silent trap of placing our hope in earthly things. After all, they seem like things we can have right now. We can see them, touch them, experience them, hold on to them. Can you think of anything that you might put your hope or trust in? What might be some earthly hopes you have?

For you, it might be putting your hope in a sport: "If I don't make the football team, I won't fit in at school."

Or maybe it's hope in your schoolwork: "I got a C instead of an A on my test. I guess I'm not very smart."

Maybe it's even putting all your hope in a person: "Being friends with Joe will make me popular at school."

But the Bible tells us something better to hope in and to hope for. So, what is worth our hope?

Jesus is our only hope, and it is through Jesus that we have the promise of eternal life (living forever with Jesus in heaven). Our hope is not something we can see or touch or experience or hold—except perhaps in brief glimpses and the promises of Scripture. No one can tell us what it is like to be glorified (made perfect!) in heaven with our Savior. We must wait patiently for our forever hope. And yet we wait as people who know the end of the story is going to be good. We wait with a trustworthy hope. And we know that our everlasting, true, and pure Hope will never let us down or put us to shame (Rom. 5:5).

LET'S GO DEEPER

1. What are earthly things or people you are tempted (or have been tempted) to put your hope in? Why will these things ultimately let you down?

2. What are some reasons we might find it hard to wait for and hope in the Lord? You can be honest.

_____

_____

_____

_____

3. What does "we know the end of the story" mean? What is the end of the story?

_____

_____

_____

_____

4. What aspects of Jesus' character assure us that He will never let us down, and we can hope in Him? For example, Jesus loves us so much. His love isn't like our love. His love is perfect! Because of His perfect love, we can trust that He will never do anything to hurt or harm us, and we can hope in Him.

_____

_____

_____

_____

PRAY

Praise God for who He is and thank Him that He is your heavenly Father. Ask God to do good things (whatever you wish to ask). Ask the Lord to help you understand what you are reading. Tell Jesus how you would like to grow (example: _Help me to be kind and forgive me for when I'm unkind_). Thank Jesus for all that He has done.

OUR HELP IN WEAKNESS

Write out Romans 8:26.

We've learned a lot about the Spirit. We've already learned that He is our helper, but here we see a very specific way the Spirit helps us.

Read the text again. How does the Spirit help us?

During a terribly sad situation, I experienced the kind of help that we see in this text. A friend of our family was very sick. Have you ever seen someone get hurt or feel sad? Maybe you've gotten sick or felt sad before and didn't know what to say or how to share why you were so sad. When I saw my friend, I found myself completely and totally without words. I was too sad and couldn't think of anything to say. I know my own kids have experienced this. When they were younger, they'd cry and sometimes have a hard time talking, but they always loved it when I would hug them.

Sometimes our pain or confusion is so deep, we can't find words to express it—to others or to God. Have you ever experienced something that made you so sad that you cried but couldn't speak? When you *can* speak, you can always ask God for help.

But, according to the Bible, we don't have to have the right words to say. When we are unable to find the words or even clear thoughts to pray in our heads, we can come to Him as we are, and the Holy Spirit will pray on our behalf.

Isn't it good news that we don't have to be perfect or have perfect words when we go to the Lord? We don't need to try to be stronger than we are to come to the Lord. He invites us to come to Him in our weakness.

Don't hesitate to call on His name, even if all you can say or think is "Jesus help me."

LET'S GO DEEPER

1. Have you ever had a difficult experience that left you speechless?

---

2. When we think of weakness, we often think of not having physical strength. After reading the lesson, what type of weakness do you think Paul is talking about?

---

3. *Do you ever feel as if you must have certain words ready before you pray to God? Why or why not?*

_____

_____

_____

_____

PRAY

Praise God for who He is and thank Him that He is your heavenly Father. Ask God to do good things (whatever you wish to ask). Ask the Lord to help you understand what you are reading. Tell Jesus how you would like to grow (example: *Help me to be kind and forgive me for when I'm unkind*). Thank Jesus for all that He has done.

INTERCEDING ACCORDING TO HIS WILL

READ ROMANS 8:27

Write out Romans 8:27.

_____

_____

_____

_____

What do you think Romans 8:27 means?

_____

_____

_____

_____

Have you ever had a tough time praying to God? When we just don't know what to say or ask, the Holy Spirit prays for us with the exact request that the Lord will answer YES to because it is "according to the will of God."[2] "According to His will" means it is exactly what God wants, and it is exactly what we need. That's why in the Lord's Prayer we pray: "Your will be done." We are telling the Lord that we trust Him to do whatever is best.

Sometimes we don't know what to pray because we are too sad. When we are so sad we don't have words, we can trust that God understands exactly what we need. When we are confused and don't know

---

2. Wayne Grudem, gen. ed., *ESV Study Bible* (Wheaton, IL: Crossway, 2008), 2171 (note on Romans 8:27).

what to ask, we can trust that He knows our needs and is listening to the Spirit. This means you can go to God any time, in any way. You don't have to have the perfect words to say!

I don't know about you, but that makes me want to run to my heavenly Father. Maybe we can go to Him and simply pray, "Lord, I don't know what to say or what is best or how to fix this. But I know You know, and so I ask You now to help me however You choose, according to Your will."

Right now, if you don't feel like you have the right words to say to the Lord, go to Him and say, "Lord, I love You and thank You for who You are." Let the Spirit say the rest to God for you. Even the prayers you don't know how to pray are reaching Him, and He will respond in love.

LET'S GO DEEPER

1. Have you ever had a hard time knowing what to pray? What did you do?

_____

_____

_____

_____

2. Why do you think it can be hard to pray sometimes?

_____

_____

_____

_____

3. Have you ever considered that the Holy Spirit is praying for you?

_____

_____

_____

4. Why do you think the Spirit is able to pray with the exact prayer needed and according to God's will?

_____

_____

_____

_____

WEEK

FIVE

START HERE: OUR ASSURANCE

READ ROMANS 8:28–30

We're waiting for the day we will be with Jesus in heaven forever, but we know the promise that everything He does on earth *now* is good. God is good, and we can trust Him completely. He thought of us before He made the world! God is making us to be more like Jesus, and it's a free gift of His grace. Jesus makes us right before God—He saves us! Jesus took all our sin, and you and I are justified (declared righteous and made clean) because of this payment. He views us just as if we've always obeyed Him.

Because of the short Scripture reading this week, continue reading in Day 1.

ALL THINGS FOR OUR GOOD

READ ROMANS 8:28

Write out Romans 8:28.

_____

_____

_____

_____

When you think of the word *good*, what do you think of? Now list ways that someone has been good to you (examples: a friend shared a piece of gum; your parents told you they loved you; your sister hugged you after you got hurt).

In this verse, we see that God is always doing good things for us. Sometimes it's through the kindness of others. Usually, when we think of good things, we also think of happiness. In other words, we might think that God is only good and doing good things in our lives when everything feels right or makes us happy. But did you know that God is good and doing good things in your life even when you feel sad or when things are hard?

Have you ever had a fight with a friend? I remember a time when I thought everything was going my way, but then I had a fight with a friend. It made me so sad. But God had a good plan. His plan was to help me grow more like Jesus, which is good. I learned how to forgive. I learned how to say "I'm sorry." I learned how to pray and ask God for help. My friend and I didn't become best friends again and that's okay. Sometimes God brings new friends. He knows what is best, so we can trust Him. It was all for my good.

The "good" that the apostle Paul writes about in Romans 8:28 could mean different things because Paul doesn't fully tell us what he means. What we do know is that the sentences around this verse talk about the Spirit speaking to God for us, Jesus' work in saving us, and our ultimate well-being in knowing Jesus. Because of these things, Paul is likely not talking about material rewards or pleasures (such as toys, clothes, or even food). Instead, the good that God does is from the Spirit's work in our lives. Ultimately, what is good is the way the Lord helps us become more like Jesus. That good work takes place in our hearts as we walk with Him.

You can trust that God is doing good things in your life. He knows everything and is absolutely working all things for the good of those who love Him. He is not withholding good from you. It isn't in His character to do so. Even what might seem hard will one day be revealed as His ultimate good in your life.

LET'S GO DEEPER

1. Have you ever experienced something that seemed terrible at the time but then turned out to be good? What was it?

_____

_____

_____

_____

2. Do you believe that God is good? List the ways God is good.

_____

_____

_____

_____

_____

_____

3. We reviewed the idea that God does good things and can even work the difficult things out for the good of those who love him. Read verse 28 again. Can you write it in your own words?

_____

_____

_____

_____

_____

_____

PRAY

Praise God for who He is and thank Him that He is your heavenly Father. Ask God to do good things (whatever you wish to ask). Ask the Lord to help you understand what you are reading. Tell Jesus how you would like to grow (example: _Help me to be kind and forgive me for when I'm unkind_). Thank Jesus for all that He has done.

GOD KNOWS US

Write out Romans 8:29.

_____

_____

_____

_____

Think of someone who knows you really well. Maybe it's a sibling or a parent. Maybe you have a best friend that you share everything with.

For me that person is my husband. There's likely no one on this earth who knows me like my husband does. But God knows me better than anyone, even better than I know myself. God knows all of history—the beginning and the end. He knows _my_ history too—and yours.

This is good news for all of us, because it means God does not do things based on what we do. He already knows. Therefore, His decision to rescue us isn't based on our good works or our faith or on anything we do. He rescues us based on the work of a God who knew us in advance. He knew us before the world was made (Eph. 1:4).

In our earthly relationships, how we are valued or loved is often a result of how we act or, even worse, what we can do for or give to others. Not so with God. We are deeply loved and valued no matter what. We are chosen because of His great love, and that love will last forever.

Why will all things work together for our good? Because He foreknew us.

1. Open your Bible and read Psalm 139:1–6 and Romans 8:27. What do these verses tell us about God and how much He knows us?

_____

_____

_____

_____

_____

2. Grab your Bible, and read Psalm 90:4, Psalm 102:12, and Isaiah 40:10. What do these verses tell us about God and how much He knows about history and the world?

_____

_____

_____

_____

_____

3. How might being known by God in advance bring peace and joy?

_____

_____

_____

_____

_____

_____

4. *God knows everything about us (even the sinful things), and yet because of Jesus, He still loves us. How does knowing this help you to love others too?*

_____

_____

_____

_____

_____

Praise God for who He is and thank Him that He is your heavenly Father. Ask God to do good things (whatever you wish to ask). Ask the Lord to help you understand what you are reading. Tell Jesus how you would like to grow (example: *Help me to be kind and forgive me for when I'm unkind*). Thank Jesus for all that He has done.

BECOMING LIKE JESUS

READ ROMANS 8:29

Write out Romans 8:29.

_____

_____

Oh, man! I did it again. I got angry and said something I regretted. I lost control of my tongue, blurted out exactly what was on my mind, and ended up hurting someone.

Same situation, but a few years later: Oh, man! I did it again. I got angry and almost said something I would regret. Although I didn't say it, I sure said a lot in my mind. I wanted to say it, but self-control enabled me not to say it out loud.

Same situation, but a few years after that: Oh, man! I did it again. I got angry, but thankfully I was able to quickly pray and ask the Lord to give me peace and self-control. By the grace and mercy of God, I was able to take my thoughts captive and didn't lash out, either verbally or in my mind.

* * * * *

When you become a Christian, a miracle happens! You are new creations. Of course, you are still you, but you are now living for Jesus and have His Spirit in you! It's a mystery, but it's true. But Christians are not yet perfect. We have simply begun the process of becoming like Christ. And because we are human, it will be hard at times not to sin. We will sin. Then we will have to ask God for forgiveness and repent (turn away from our sin) time and time again.

Have you ever done something that was wrong or bad and you knew better? In Romans 7:19, the apostle Paul wrote about the "wrestling" we experience: "For I do not do the good I want, but the evil I do not want is what I keep on doing." We try to do the right thing and then mess up. Or we know we should do the right thing but do the wrong thing anyway. We need God's help to obey Him! When He helps us see that we've done something wrong, and we begin to change, that is called sanctification.

Sanctification is simply the process of becoming more like Jesus. In Philippians 1:6, Paul also tells us of God's promise to finish the good work He has begun in us. In other words, there's work yet to do in us, and there will be work to do until the day we are made perfect in heaven and with Christ.

Sanctification may feel like the scenes I shared at the beginning of this lesson. Take anger, for example. You probably won't stop being angry, but you can become quicker to realize you are getting angry and quicker to say no to it. And when you do sin, you can become quicker to respond to your sin by confessing (telling God and your parent or guardian) and asking for forgiveness.

Sanctification is a lifelong process. As long as we are following Jesus, we will be growing more and more like Him. God's Spirit is at work in your heart even now.

> **LET'S GO DEEPER**

1. Open your Bible and look up 2 Corinthians 5:17. What happens after you accept Jesus as your Lord and Savior?

---

2. *We talked a lot about sanctification. Do you remember what it means? Write it out in your own words.*

_____

_____

_____

3. *Why do you think becoming more like Jesus is an important part of the Christian life?*

_____

_____

_____

4. *Is there anything you struggle with (anger, fear, jealousy, gossip)? Write out Galatians 5:22–23. These are ways we can grow more like Jesus.*

_____

_____

_____

_____

5. *I shared a few practical steps to help you and me grow more like Jesus. Do you remember what they are? (Hint: confess.)*

_____

_____

_____

PRAY

Praise God for who He is and thank Him that He is your heavenly Father. Ask God to do good things (whatever you wish to ask). Ask the Lord to help you understand what you are reading. Tell Jesus how you would like to grow (example: *Help me to be kind and forgive me for when I'm unkind*). Thank Jesus for all that He has done.

YOU WERE CALLED
TO SALVATION

READ ROMANS 8:30

Write out Romans 8:30.

Have you ever been in a deep sleep and then someone woke you up? Do you remember how it felt? Maybe you jumped. Maybe you rolled back over in your bed trying to get one more minute of sleep. Perhaps you are like me and you love the morning, so you stretched a little and welcomed the wake-up call. Sometimes we wake up on our own, but often we need someone or something else to get us out of our deep sleep. There was never a greater awakening than the moment we accepted Jesus as Savior.

You and I were dead in our sins (Eph. 2:1). God sought us and called us into salvation. Here's another example: Have you ever worked on a math problem and just didn't understand it at all? When I was young, math was a very difficult subject for me. But then one day it clicked, and I understood. You know how that math problem you didn't understand suddenly makes sense? Similarly, when we are called, God makes the gospel clear to us. It clicks!

When we are called by God to salvation, it clicks. We understand what the good news means. We get it. That doesn't mean we know everything, but it does mean that we now really know Jesus.

1. Do you remember when the gospel clicked? Write about what happened or tell someone about it.

_____

_____

_____

_____

2. Sometimes we forget the moment God called us to Himself and we answered. We need to remember it! Why do you think it's good to remember that God called us to live for Him?

_____

_____

_____

_____

3. Why do you think remembering that can help us be thankful for God?

_____

_____

_____

_____

PRAY

Praise God for who He is and thank Him that He is your heavenly Father. Ask God to do good things (whatever you wish to ask). Ask the Lord to help you understand what you are reading. Tell Jesus how you would like to grow (example: _Help me to be kind and forgive me for when I'm unkind_). Thank Jesus for all that He has done.

JUST AS IF YOU'VE ALWAYS OBEYED

READ ROMANS 8:30

Write out Romans 8:30.

_____

_____

_____

When I was younger, I wanted to be a lawyer. I loved learning about legal things and watching television shows about lawyers in a courtroom setting. Although I didn't become a lawyer, I *am* grateful for one legal word I learned when I got older.

The word is *justification*. For Christians, it's an important word! It's a legal term that means we are in right and good standing before the Lord. When we are justified before God, we have traded in our unrighteousness (sin and wickedness) for Jesus' righteousness (all His goodness). We are only righteous (or just) before God through the work and person of Jesus Christ.

I've heard this explained in different ways. Here is one: Once you have been justified, God views you as if you never sinned or as if you had always obeyed. Think about that! It means that God doesn't look at you and see only the bad things you've done. Instead, He looks at you and sees all the good things *Jesus* has done. That's pretty amazing, considering we not only *have* sinned and deserve the full punishment for it, but we *continue* to sin. Being justified, then, is an unspeakably generous, kind, and merciful gift of God's grace. It's also a picture of what we have to look forward to in the next life—glorification.

Before we move on to another new word, can you define justification? *Put it in your own words.*

_____

_____

_____

Even though we have been justified, there is still a big difference between who we are *now* and who we *will* be when we are with Jesus. On this earth, we may increasingly be able to obey God, follow Him, and rest in Him, but we will never once do any of it perfectly.

This shouldn't cause us to give up or be sad. After all, we don't obey God because we will earn favor before Him; we obey out of love and worship for Him. But it helps to remember that we have something greater to look forward to. One day, we *will* be perfect just as Christ is perfect (1 Cor. 15:49). One day we will be glorified—completely free of sin, completely made holy.

It's impossible to describe this glorious truth with words. It's unimaginable. Here's how God, through His Word, describes that future to His children now: "What we will be has not yet appeared; but . . . when [Jesus] appears we shall be like him, because we shall see him as he is" (1 John 3:2). The Bible is incredibly clear that one day we will not only be with Christ, we will be *like* Christ. We will be glorified.

What does glorification mean? Write it in your own words.

_____

_____

_____

Knowing that one day we will be perfect—our future glorification— should motivate us to love, obey, and serve our Lord every day. God is worthy of our worship because He is God. But the fact that He is good and gracious and has promised to glorify us helps us run to Him all the more.

1. Open your Bible and look up 2 Corinthians 5:21. What does it say? Now think of the word justification. How does this verse help you understand that word?

_____

_____

_____

_____

2. What is the difference between justification and glorification? Why might it be important to not mix up the two words?

_____

_____

_____

_____

3. How does knowing that one day you will be perfect (glorification) help you obey Jesus today?

_____

_____

_____

_____

4. How does understanding our justification help motivate us to live for Christ today?

_____

_____

_____

_____

Praise God for who He is and thank Him that He is your heavenly Father. Ask God to do good things (whatever you wish to ask). Ask the Lord to help you understand what you are reading. Tell Jesus how you would like to grow (example: *Help me to be kind and forgive me for when I'm unkind*). Thank Jesus for all that He has done.

WEEK SIX

START HERE:
EVERLASTING LOVE

READ ROMANS 8:31–39

What do we say about all these things we've learned over the past five weeks about God, His Son, His Spirit, and His everlasting love for us? It can all be summarized in Paul's unforgettable words: "If God is for us, who can be against us?" *God is for us!*

If God could give His only Son for our sakes, then we can and should rest in the grace and assurance of our trustworthy Father's words to us. If we are in Christ, nothing can—or will—ever separate us from our Savior. What joy. What peace. What security.

This week we will finish off our study with some incredible news and assurance of our faith. Don't be intimidated by the number of questions in the "Respond" section. This isn't a test. It *is* a great way to discover all the treasure stored in the last nine verses of Romans 8. I think you'll find the questions chock-full of the good news of the gospel. So, let's dig in and see if we can answer them all.

Because of the short Scripture reading this week, continue reading in Day 1.

IF GOD IS FOR US . . .

READ ROMANS 8:31

Write out Romans 8:31.

In the part of the United States where I live (Hello! The South), it's not unusual to see or be exposed to Bible verses every day. If you don't see one written on a car bumper sticker or taped to the back of a car, then you'll likely see one hanging on the wall of a restaurant. As an adult, I see Scripture on mugs, T-shirts, and pretty designed squares posted on social media. But I sometimes wonder if those of us who post those verses on social media, wear them, or even repeat them actually *know* them.

I'm not talking about the context of the verses or their interpretation. I mean, do we know the Author of the Word? Do we know God? Do we know His Son? And if we know Him, do we truly believe Him?

The verse we are exploring today is one of the most quoted verses in the entire Bible. The question Paul asks here summarizes all we've learned about our great salvation since the beginning of chapter 8. But the verse doesn't necessarily stop there. This verse is the climax of the first half of the book of Romans. We might even say that when Paul writes of "these things," he's referring to everything from chapters 5 through 8 . . . or even to the first half of the book. Thinking on the truths and blessings Paul has been teaching in his letter reminds you and me that we have such eternal security with Jesus. He is awesome!

But let's look at the verse just before Romans 8:31. That verse gives us reason to rejoice too. Think about "all these things" we've learned while reading Romans 8:30: God chose us, invited us to come to Him, gave us right standing with Him, and will one day make us perfect. We are not second thoughts in the mind and heart of God. Before He made the world, He had us in mind.

Here is just a taste of what we know about God:

- He is all powerful: "For nothing will be impossible with God" (Luke 1:37).

- He is unchanging: "For I the Lord do not change; therefore you, O children of Jacob, are not consumed" (Mal. 3:6).

- He is all knowing: "Great is our Lord, and abundant in power; his understanding is beyond measure" (Ps. 147:5).

- He is holy (set apart and absolutely pure): "And one called to another and said: 'Holy, holy, holy is the Lord of hosts; the whole earth is full of his glory!'" (Isa. 6:3).

The message of Romans 8 is that God, who is awesome in every way, is on our side. That doesn't mean we won't experience hard times or opposition, such as from other people, from Satan, and even from our own doubts that God loves. (So, we need to ask God to help us believe it!) But those challenges are defeated by what we have in Christ Jesus.

Think about that! Not only is God on our side, He has also made a way for us to know Him deeply through salvation and His Son. If this is who God is (there's so much more to learn about Him), and we know just a little of all He has done (we'll spend forever learning more) . . . if this is the God who is *for* us, who then really can be against us?

No one!

1. Do you remember Week 1 in our study? Look back. What ideas from Romans 5 might be similar to the fact that God is for us?

2. Why might thinking about who God is (His character or attributes) give us reason for awe and provide us with a sense of security?

3. Have you ever felt like you were opposed by someone? Without gossiping (that is, naming the person or, worse, talking bad about him or her), explain how their opposition made you feel. Now that you know that God is for you, how might that change your response to hard things?

4. How does God show that He is for us?

Praise God for who He is and thank Him that He is your heavenly Father. Ask God to do good things (whatever you wish to ask). Ask the Lord to help you understand what you are reading. Tell Jesus how you would like to grow (example: *Help me to be kind and forgive me for when I'm unkind*). Thank Jesus for all that He has done.

WILL HE NOT GRACIOUSLY GIVE US ALL THINGS?

Write out Romans 8:32.

_____

_____

Have you ever thought about the words of John 3:16? Look it up in your Bible.

Jesus is the Son of God. God loved the world so much that He gave up His Son for the world. Because of what Jesus has done, you and I can have a relationship with God. This isn't new news. We've been studying about the gospel for the past five weeks. We see it here again, so we can remember this *good* news.

Remembering that God sent His one and only Son to die for us, Paul asks an important question in Romans 8:32: "He who did not spare his own Son but gave him up for us all, how will he not also with him graciously give us all things?" There is no greater sacrifice than for a parent to give up a child—nothing. If God was willing to sacrifice His Son for us, why would we ever doubt anything else that God says or does? Why would we not trust His promise to give us "all things"?

What do you think God means by "all things"?

_____

_____

_____

_____

Although I do believe that "all things" in our text refers to both physical and spiritual needs, this doesn't mean that God is going to give us everything we *want*. Second Peter 1:3 helps us understand what Paul likely means by telling us that God's power has "granted to us all things that pertain to life and godliness." In other words, God will provide all we *need*, and ultimately what we need most is a right relationship with God. That's exactly what God has provided through His Son. There is nothing we need that God hasn't already taken care of for us. Praise God!

You and I may sometimes have to try hard to believe this. It's easy to say, but not to live out. We may sometimes need to pray, as yet another loving father once cried out to Jesus, "I believe; help my unbelief!" (Mark 9:24). And the Lord understands this. He knows we sometimes struggle to believe Him, which is why He reminds us repeatedly through His Word to trust Him.

You can say this, and it is true: "If God is for us"—and sent His only Son to die on a cross on our behalf—"who can be against us?"

LET'S GO DEEPER

1. Read John 3:16 again. Write it out in your own words.

_____

_____

_____

_____

2. Why is it important to know that God sent His Son, Jesus, for us?

_____

_____

_____

_____

3. How does knowing that God sent His Son help you love and worship Jesus?

_____

_____

_____

_____

4. How does knowing that God sent His Son help you believe that God will give you everything you need?

_____

_____

_____

_____

5. Do you believe that God hears your prayers and cares about all your needs?

_____

6. How does God's sacrifice prove that He really is for us?

_____

_____

_____

_____

PRAY

Praise God for who He is and thank Him that He is your heavenly Father. Ask God to do good things (whatever you wish to ask). Ask the Lord to help you understand what you are reading. Tell Jesus how you would like to grow (example: _Help me to be kind and forgive me for when I'm unkind_). Thank Jesus for all that He has done.

WHO SHALL BRING A CHARGE AGAINST GOD'S ELECT?

READ ROMANS 8:33

Write out Romans 8:33.

_____

_____

When someone does something that is wrong they are usually "charged" with a crime. So, if someone takes something from a store without paying for it, it is considered stealing. When the police find out, they will charge (or accuse) the person for the crime. The person will need to pay for their crime. They may pay for it by spending time in jail or completing community service. Sometimes, if the person who stole something is sorry for their crime, the judge may show mercy to them, and their payment or punishment is smaller.

A "charge" is a legal term. We have seen another legal term already. Do you remember what it was?

A charge is an accusation. For example, if you take a pencil from your sibling and then your sibling tells an adult, your sibling has just accused you of taking a pencil. Or maybe your sibling didn't see what happened to the pencil but thought you took it and told the adult, "He took my pencil!" when you didn't! You've just been accused of taking something you did not. You have been charged with taking the pencil! So, an accusation can be true or false.

Here in our text, Paul uses this legal term to describe the experience of being accused before God. He is asking: Who can bring a charge against God's elect? In other words, who can accuse those whom God has chosen? The answer is obviously "no one." But that doesn't mean that no one *tries* to bring charges. In fact, we are charged one way or another almost daily.

If the apostle Paul writes about someone bringing a charge, we must wonder, who brings these charges?

Who do you think brings a charge against those who know Jesus?

_____

_____

_____

Here are two examples:

The first one who tries to charge us before God is Satan, who is called "the accuser" in the Bible (Zech. 3:1; Rev. 12:10). He goes around trying to make us doubt that God is real or that His Word is true and also tries to make us feel guilty. Right before a man in the Bible named Job was stripped of all he owned, Satan accused Job of only following the Lord because of all the earthly wealth he had (Job 1:9–10). And the apostle Peter warns us how mean Satan's accusations can be: "Be sober-minded; be watchful. Your adversary the devil prowls around like a roaring lion, seeking someone to devour" (1 Peter 5:8). This adversary wants us to stand charged and guilty to the very end. He wants us to stand before the Lord defeated.

And who is the second accuser? Our own hearts!

Sometimes when we sin, we feel sad because we know it was the wrong thing to do, and we are sad because we disobeyed God. When we are sad, we turn to God and ask for His forgiveness. He always forgives us if we ask Him. When we respond to our sin that way, it is a good and godly sadness over our sin. That is called "godly grief." Godly grief means that we are sad that we disobey, and it leads us to repentance (2 Cor. 7:10).

So, how do we accuse ourselves? We accuse ourselves anytime we feel guilty and think we can't or won't be forgiven by God. We feel like we've done too much. We don't think that what Jesus did on the cross for us was enough. We may never say this out loud, but our response shows us that we feel too guilty to ask God for forgiveness. So, instead, we might try to hide our sin (not telling anyone that we did something wrong). We might also beat ourselves up about it, begging for forgiveness but never trusting that we are forgiven. This is false guilt and "worldly sorrow" that grows out of the thought that we must perform for the approval of God, that failure is unacceptable, and that sin is unforgivable.

Worldly sorrow sounds like the opposite of good news, doesn't it?

Here's some good news: none of those accusations carry any weight before God—not if we are in Christ! Remember, if you belong to Jesus, God is for you, and no one can truly be against you. Whoever accuses us—even ourselves—and whatever charges are brought against us, we can rest in knowing that it is God who judges, and those God has chosen and Jesus died for are justified before the Lord. We are the same people Jesus will one day present as perfect to His Father (Eph. 5:27). None of the charges against us before God can stick.

What incredible news! Your standing before the Lord cannot be overthrown. Not by Satan, the accuser, and not by your own heart.

If God is for you, who can be against you?

No one and nothing.

LET'S GO DEEPER

1. Look up Zechariah 3:1 in the Old Testament and Revelation 12:10 in the New Testament. What do they say about Satan?

---

2. Have you ever felt charged with something, either by Satan or your own heart? What was it?

3. Why is it important to remember that we have an accuser (Satan)?

4. Have you felt the kind of false guilt or worldly sorrow described above? How can you tell the difference between this and true godly grief?

5. How does a right view of sin and a right view of guilt actually help us tell Jesus what we did?

Praise God for who He is and thank Him that He is your heavenly Father. Ask God to do good things (whatever you wish to ask). Ask the Lord to help you understand what you are reading. Tell Jesus how you would like to grow (example: *Help me to be kind and forgive me for when I'm unkind*). Thank Jesus for all that He has done.

WHO IS TO CONDEMN?

Write out Romans 8:34.

_____

_____

_____

_____

My mom used to say that she felt like a "broken record." She was referring to the old vinyl recordings. If a vinyl disk is scratched or broken, the needle will skip and repeat the last thing it played over and over again. Mom felt like that when she had to remind us repeatedly what we needed to do, only to have us forget what she said—or (let's be honest) ignore it.

Today, as a parent, I can see exactly how my mom felt. I will tell my children something, and five minutes later, I'll have to tell them again. I don't (usually) get angry that I must repeat myself, but I do get frustrated and think, "Don't you understand yet? Aren't you listening?"

I'm thankful that the Lord is not like me and that He is pure and patient. And yet I wonder if Paul was thinking, "Don't you get it yet?" when he wrote this verse. These words bring Romans 8 full circle because they tell us, again, that no one can condemn us if we are in Christ. When a word is repeated in the Bible, we must pay attention. There is a reason we need to be reminded that there is no condemnation for those in Christ Jesus.

Do you remember studying the word condemnation *at the beginning of our study on Romans 8? What does condemnation mean? Feel free to turn back and review your notes.*

Maybe we need the reminder because, like children, we will forget two minutes after we are told. Our hearts will attempt to condemn us every time we sin. But as 1 John 3:20–21 reminds us, "Whenever our heart condemns us, God is greater than our heart, and he knows everything. Beloved, if our heart does not condemn us, we have confidence before God."

Paul's answer to his own question—"Who is to condemn?"—is also worth repeating over and over and over. Why don't we need to worry about being condemned? Because "Christ Jesus is the one who died— more than that, who was raised—who is at the right hand of God, who indeed is interceding for us" (Rom. 8:34).

Jesus died for our sins, and we stand right before God; therefore, no one can condemn us.

Jesus defeated death and is at the most powerful position in the universe—the right hand of God; therefore, no one can condemn us.

And Jesus is praying right now for you and for me (Heb. 7:25). The whole gospel—the good news—gives us confidence that no one can condemn us.

It's a truth we can trust: no one can condemn us because our Savior lives.

1. *Have you ever struggled with* condemnation? *Why is it such a serious problem?*

_____

_____

_____

_____

2. *Ultimately, when we feel condemned, we are forgetting the gospel. What are some ways you can remind yourself of the gospel daily?*

_____

_____

_____

_____

3. *Why is Jesus' resurrection so important to the message of this chapter and to our faith?*

_____

_____

_____

_____

4. *Why is Jesus' position in heaven—seated at the right hand of God, right next to His Father—important?*

_____

_____

_____

_____

5. *Notice that Romans 8 says that both the Spirit (vv. 26–27) and Jesus (v. 34) intercede on our behalf. In what ways are these intercessions alike? Different? What is your response to knowing that both the Holy Spirit and the Son of God are actively involved in connecting you with the Father?*

PRAY

Praise God for who He is and thank Him that He is your heavenly Father. Ask God to do good things (whatever you wish to ask). Ask the Lord to help you understand what you are reading. Tell Jesus how you would like to grow (example: *Help me to be kind and forgive me for when I'm unkind*). Thank Jesus for all that He has done.

THE LAST GREAT LESSON: WHO SHALL SEPARATE US?

Write out Romans 8:35–39.

_____

_____

_____

_____

_____

_____

_____

_____

_____

_____

_____

_____

Here we are at Paul's fifth and final question—really a series of questions—the culmination of the life-giving encouragement in chapter 8. And now for the first time we see that it's all about love: "the love of God in Christ Jesus." Everything that we have been learning has been wrapped up in this perfect love. Every act of God is motivated by His love for us. God's love is the surety of His staying power—His love is everlasting.

But there are times when we doubt God's love for us. So, Paul asks a series of questions to make sure we know how faithful God's love is.

In those questions, Paul lists: trouble, pain, persecution, hunger, poverty, danger, and threats. Can any of these things separate us from the love of Christ?

Here are the answers using the words of Jesus:

Trouble or pain or persecution? Jesus says to us, "I have said these things to you, that in me you may have peace. In the world you will have tribulation. But take heart; I have overcome the world" (John 16:33). In our troubles and trials, we can be calm because we know that God is with us. We know that He is *for* us, and that Jesus gives us His peace.

Hunger or poverty? Jesus says, "If God so clothes the grass of the field, which today is alive and tomorrow is thrown into the oven, will he not much more clothe you?" (Matt. 6:30). God provides for all our needs. He doesn't promise us riches, but He does promise to take care of us. Neither hunger nor poverty can separate us from the love of Christ.

Danger or threats? We may ask during scary times, "Where are You, Lord?" But the Lord will surely answer, "Right here." Jesus tells of His everlasting love through danger or sword: "Don't be afraid of those who want to kill your body; they cannot touch your soul. Fear only God, who can destroy both soul and body in hell. What is the price of two sparrows—one copper coin? But not a single sparrow can fall to the ground without your Father knowing it. And the very hairs on your head are all numbered. So don't be afraid; you are more valuable to God than a whole flock of sparrows" (Matt.10:28–31 NLT).

Because we know that Jesus is for us and nothing will ever separate us from Him, we can say: "Victory is ours!" How are we victorious? "Through him who loved us" (Rom. 8:37). We are not victorious because of anything in or about us. We are victorious because of God's love for us.

Read Roman 8:38–39. Write it in your own words.

_____

_____

_____

_____

_____

_____

These last two sentences remind us that we can have confidence that all this is true because of the character of God. Remember at the beginning of the week on Day 1 when we reviewed all the wonderful things about God? It is because of who He is that nothing—absolutely nothing!—can cut us off from the love of God in Christ Jesus.

Not one thing we might think could separate us from God will be able to. And that is the reality of our victory. We are victorious in the faithful and everlasting love of Christ Jesus.

His love will never fail, will never let go, and will never allow us to be trampled. God will be faithful to us to the very end of time. With confidence and great assurance of faith, we can proclaim from the mountaintops: God is *for* us!

LET'S GO DEEPER

1. Sometimes when really hard things happen to us and we suffer, we think that God is upset with us. But as Romans 8 helps us understand, God always loves us, and nothing can separate us from His love. Why is it good to remember that God loves you when bad things happen to you?

_____

_____

_____

_____

2. Can you think of other places in the Bible where you see a focus on the love of Jesus? If your Bible has a concordance, index, or list of words in the back of it, look up the word love. Write down any Scripture verses that mention the love of Jesus—as many as you can. Then take note of what is surrounding those texts (the scene, other text, what the writer is addressing). What did you learn about Jesus' love from this brief word study?

3. How are we victorious in Jesus?

4. *Sum it all up. Why can we say with confidence that God is for us?*

_____

_____

_____

_____

_____

_____

PRAY

Praise God for who He is and thank Him that He is your heavenly Father. Ask God to do good things (whatever you wish to ask). Ask the Lord to help you understand what you are reading. Tell Jesus how you would like to grow (example: *Help me to be kind and forgive me for when I'm unkind*). Thank Jesus for all that He has done.

WHAT WILL YOU DISCOVER NEXT ABOUT GOD?

I'm older and have been a Christian for many years, but you know what? I'm still learning about God! You and I get to spend our whole lives learning more about our Lord and Savior. You have just spent the past six weeks learning all about God's unfailing love. Here's something exciting: you can study the Bible! You did it! Don't stop with this Bible study. Use the Read, Observe, Interpret, and Apply method you learned to study another book of the Bible and continue growing in your relationship with God.

Here's a reminder of what you can do:

READ: I encourage you to begin your study of any part of the Bible by simply reading it that way—like a book. Feel free to write down certain themes you see, repeated words, and words you don't understand, but don't get bogged down in the details.

OBSERVE: Ask questions like who, what, when, where, and why—Who is the author writing to? What is happening during that time or in the passage? When was it written? Where was it written and where was the letter sent? Why was the letter written? Write out your answers.

INTERPRET: What does the text mean? Summarize it in your own words. Look for repeated words and then look up the meaning of any words you may not know. What's the context? Is there anything about the book of Romans that you've learned that will help you understand the meaning of the chapter? What did you learn in Day 1 or 2 that might help you understand why Paul wrote this chapter? How does it relate to the rest of Scripture? Is there anything that you've read in your Bible that reminds you of this chapter? What does the text say about God or about Jesus? Write out your answers.

APPLY: What is God's Word saying for me today? Write out your answer and pray for the Lord's help to do what you have learned.